MW01005945

IT IS TIME FOR
YOU
TO BE
FINANCIALLY
FREE!

Patricia Diane Cota-Robles

New Age Study of Humanity's Purpose
P.O. Box 41883
Tucson, AZ 85717
Phone 520-885-7909, Fax 520-751-3835

New Age Study of Humanity's Purpose, Inc.
PO Box 41883
Tucson, AZ 85717
Phone 520-885-7909
Fax 520-751-3835

Cover by Sharon Maia Nichols
All Rights Reserved
Printed in the United States of America

ISBN: 0-9615287-6-1
FIRST PRINTING OCTOBER 18, 1997

Prayer for Gratitude and Acceptance

*Through the Power of God anchored in my Heart and within the Hearts of ALL Humanity, I invoke the Divine Flames of Gratitude and Acceptance. Precious Sacred Fire, blaze in, through and around every electron of my Being. Flood my consciousness with Gratitude **for** and the Acceptance **of** God's Limitless Flow of Abundance. Lift me into the Realms of Truth, and Bless me with the clear Inner Knowing that the God Supply of all good things is my Divine Birthright.*

I relinquish now, in the Name of God, all of the power I have ever given to lack and limitation through my thoughts, words, actions or feelings.

I relinquish now, in the Name of God, all of the beliefs I have ever had that are based in poverty consciousness.

In deep Humility and Gratitude I consecrate and dedicate my very life to be the open door through which God's Limitless Abundance will flow to Bless me, my family, friends, co-workers and ALL Humanity.

As I think, speak, feel and act, the Presence of God within me is expanding God's Gift of Prosperity to all life evolving on Earth.

I AM an Awakened Light Being!

*I Gratefully Accept God's Gift
of Prosperity
and Limitless Abundance!*

And So It Is!

I AM! I AM! I AM!

THANK YOU!!!

Words cannot express the Gratitude we at the New Age Study of Humanity's Purpose have for the generous Love Offerings you have sent to support our work.

Through your mental, emotional, Spiritual and financial gifts, we have been able to continue offering our seminars for FREE.

Making the Sacred Knowledge that is pouring forth from the Realms of Illumined Truth available to ALL Humanity, without having to limit people by charging a fee, is the greatest service we can possibly render.

As One Unified Heart, we invoke our Father-Mother God and the entire Company of Heaven to expand your precious Love Offerings a thousand-times a thousand-fold as they return to you.

God Bless you for your service to the Light!

May the perpetual flow of God's Limitless Abundance expand daily and hourly as It tangibly manifests in **your** life and the lives of ALL Humanity.

And So It Is!

I AM! I AM! I AM!

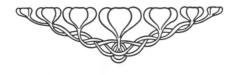

The New Age Study of Humanity's Purpose, Inc., is a non-profit, educational organization. We have a 501 (c) 3 tax deductible status for contributions and financial donations. Thank you!

iv

ABUNDANCE
IS OUR DIVINE BIRTHRIGHT

Abundance is our Divine Birthright, and circumstances are now perfect for us to reclaim our God-given heritage of prosperity.

In the 1980s, we reached into the depths of lack and limitation. People began to believe that America and the World were in a state of decline.

It was a very unique time on Earth, often a confusing and frightening time. Through the advancement of modern technology we had instant Global communication, and we were constantly being informed of the extreme imbalances appearing on the screen of life. We saw lack and limitation manifesting everywhere. We saw hunger, homelessness and all manner of poverty. We heard dire reports of economic failure, such as the demise of the savings and loan companies and the crash of the stock market. The terms foreclosure, bankruptcy and recession became household words. Companies went out of business daily, and the jobless rate increased. There was a prevailing sense of uncertainty and fear that ran through all economic circles and the general public as well. This sense of fear created a consciousness of panic that caused people to cast caution to the wind, and the insidious influence of greed and selfishness tightened its paralyzing grip. When that occurred, integrity and social conscience were swept aside. The environment was ignored, and the well-being of Humanity and the Earth Herself were jeopardized in pursuit of the almighty dollar. From outer appearances it looked as if the economy was "*going to hell in a handbasket*," but nothing could have been further from the Truth.

In actuality, the negative patterns of poverty, greed, corruption, selfishness, etc., were being pushed to the surface in the 1980s by the increasing influx of God's Light. The Divine Intent was to create a catalyst that would shift Humanity's consciousness and motivate people into action. It seems as though we use pain as our greatest motivator, so as we experienced the full brunt of poverty, either personally or by observing the plight of others, millions of people were inspired to invoke the Light of God to transmute and heal the maladies of lack and limitation. As Awakening Humanity invoked Light into the dire situations surfacing in people's lives, we cleared the way for *Prosperity Consciousness* to be reborn.

Now we are witnessing the initial impulse of a Global economic boom. This boom has the potential of reaching a scale never before experienced. We are in a period of sustained growth that visionary economists perceive could double the World's economy every dozen years and bring prosperity to literally *billions* of people on Earth.

Just imagine, we are standing on the threshold of an economic explosion that will do much to solve the seemingly insurmountable problem of poverty and ease tensions throughout the World.

This phenomenon is not just a fluke. It is part of a Divine Plan that is being orchestrated by God and the entire Company of Heaven as They work in harmony and unison with Awakening Humanity. This plan has been gradually unfolding for millenia. The purging that took place throughout the economic world was a necessary, critical part of the planetary transformation that is now at hand.

For aeons of time the monetary system of the World has been abused. Instead of the natural exchange of give-and-take, based on the principle of always working toward the highest good for all concerned, the wealth of the World has been used by the elite few to manipulate, dominate, oppress and control the multitudes.

Money has been such a source of pain and suffering throughout history that religious orders in both Eastern and Western cultures considered money itself to be innately evil. They, thereby, denounced it and actually took vows of poverty. This action gave the Spiritual aspirants of the World the message that somehow poverty was a virtue. Interestingly, this belief system perpetuated the schism between the haves and the have-nots. It also created a phenomenon that intensified the abuse of money. The people who were truly seeking greater levels of Truth to improve the quality of life on the Planet and those who were genuinely striving toward Spiritual growth and self-mastery were being taught by the world religions that money was evil and should not be acquired. That belief left the money in the hands of those who were not pursuing the highest good for all, but rather pursuing the self-indulgent gratification of greed and power. Because the abuse of money has been the order of the day on Earth for literally millennia, we probably all have etheric records and memories of times when we either abused our wealth or when others used their wealth to abuse us. These etheric records vibrate at a subconscious level, but they can be very effective at repelling money away from us. In either case, whether we were the abused or the abuser, or on occasion both, the message was that money is a source of pain. It is very hard to get past that subconscious block and allow money into our lives when we keep associating money with pain.

This is truly a Cosmic Moment on Earth, a moment being referred to as the dawn of the Permanent Golden Age. In this dawning Age, it has been decreed by Divine Fiat that Heaven shall manifest on Earth. As you can well imagine, poverty, homelessness, lack and limitation do not exist in Heaven. Consequently, that means that they will not exist on Earth either when the transformation is complete. But what we must realize is that those maladies are not going to be eliminated because someone waves a wand and magically makes them disappear. They are going to be eliminated because you and I and every other person evolving on Earth learn to apply the Laws of Prosperity accurately and effectively in our lives.

At any given moment our environment is reflecting a sum total of our thoughts, words, actions, feelings and beliefs. The World at large is a reflection of Humanity's consciousness. The remaining negative experiences of lack and limitation occurring in our personal lives and in the Global economy are not the result of God punishing us for our past abuse of money as some are indicating. It is merely our own energy returning to us to allow us to experience the results of our actions. At this critical time of change, if there is any area in our lives in which we are not reaching our highest potential, it is being pushed to the surface in such a way that we don't have any choice but to face it and deal with it. We are no longer being allowed by our Higher Selves to stuff or deny our problems. Needless to say, poverty is a problem, and it is surfacing in the lives of those whose thoughts, words, actions and feelings are based in poverty consciousness. As long as we are comfortable, we are willing to stagnate for-ever, but when we experience a real crisis in our lives, we frantically try to alleviate it. We strayed from the original Divine Plan as far as money goes, but we are now clearing up our past mistakes and getting back on track.

The imbalance and failure of our economic system was brought to our awareness through the media so that we could clearly see the error of our ways of greed and selfishness. Now, through greater insight and under-standing, we will create an economic system that re-flects a reverence for ALL life and the highest good for all concerned.

Abundance is actually our natural state of Being. The supply of the Universe is limitless. When the Earth was created, God provided Humanity with everything we needed to abide in this verdant paradise of splen-dor, including the knowledge and wisdom to sustain a life of prosperity and abundance. It was only when we began to use our gift of free will to express thoughts and feelings that reflected a consciousness of less than prosperity that we began to experience lack and limi-tation.

We must remember that our thoughts are creative. Whatever we put our attention and energy into, what-ever we think and feel, we bring into form. When Hu-manity began to express thoughts and feelings of fear and lack, these discordant vibrations began to reflect on the atomic substance of physical matter. Then, in-stead of the continual manifestation of the God Supply of all good things, we began to experience extreme imbalances and impoverishment. The Elemental King-dom, which always reflects Humanity's consciousness, began to show signs of decay and degeneration. Floods, famines, droughts and pestilence became the order of the day. The people evolving on Earth observed the changes taking place, and they became more fearful and confused. This negative state of consciousness perpetuated even greater degrees of lack and scarcity. Thus, over aeons of time, Humanity created a building momentum of poverty consciousness. We became deeply entrenched in the discordant thoughtforms of limitation. We observed the indigence of the outer world and accepted it as our natural state of Being. We forgot that we are Co-Creators in our Earthly experience. We lost the awareness that the things occurring in our lives are merely a reflection of our thoughts, words, feelings, actions and beliefs. Instead, we looked at the poverty of the World and tried to justify it by proclaiming it to be, of all things, God's Will. We felt victimized and tried to outsmart our so-called lot in life. We became conniving and deceitful. We believed that the only way we could have *enough* was to take things away from others. This attitude became the basis for war, crime, corruption, greed and selfishness. The momentum of poverty consciousness increased throughout the Ages, and day-by-day, we methodically sank into our present level of degradation.

If we will objectively observe the negative things occurring in the World, we will see that almost every single destructive expression of life is, in some way, reflecting a belief in lack and limitation and also reflecting the actions of greed and selfishness that naturally accompany that belief system. This material spiral into oblivion is now coming to an end. It is critical, for the survival of the Planet, that we stop our distorted acceptance of poverty and begin clearly and effectively developing a Consciousness of Prosperity. **Poverty is in absolute opposition to the Divine Plan for the Earth and all of Humanity.** Poverty cannot exist in the presence of Light, and the Earth is destined to be a Planet of Light.

OPEN UP TO THE FLOW
OF GOD'S ABUNDANCE

There are millions of souls now evolving on Earth who are awakening to the inner knowledge that recorded deep within their cellular memories is the understanding of the Laws of Prosperity. These souls know, through every fiber of their Beings, that God is their supply, and they know that supply is limitless. Yet their life experience is still reflecting signs of the lack of financial sustenance. This paradox confirms the fact that even the illumined souls on Earth who have the intellectual knowledge and wisdom of the Laws of Prosperity have powerful etheric records and memories based in poverty consciousness that *repel money away from them.*

Because of the need for money in our everyday lives just for survival, we have developed a concern and tremendous fear about it that often forms a block that prevents money from flowing into our lives. One of the most difficult things to truly believe and accept is that the supply of the Universe is limitless, and everything we need already exists. What we have to do is apply the Natural Laws that govern the abundant supply of the Universe and open up to that flow of Abundance.

In order to attain financial freedom, the first thing we must do is clear our relationship with money. We need to eliminate fear and realize that money is a source of energy, *period.* It is not some awesome entity that comes into our lives to wield its power over us and rule our destinies. It is only because of our fear that we have allowed money to have that control over us.

A great deal of the fear and confusion we have about money comes from childhood programming, misunderstandings and religious dogma. It also comes from feelings of low self-esteem and unworthiness. One of the most erroneous concepts we have is the belief that it is *Spiritual* or part of our *Divine Plan* to suffer and be poor. On the contrary, to say that poverty and lack are the *"Will of God "* is actually blasphemous.

Since not one electron of energy is sent forth from God that is less than perfect, it follows that *poverty*, which is most certainly less than perfect, has to be part of our own human miscreation. Therefore, poverty is certainly **not** the Will of God and, since it is a form of misqualified energy, it could actually be considered in religious terms as a *sin*. It is a vice. Poverty leads to all manner of crime, family problems, drug and alcohol abuse, tension, stress, high blood pressure, worry and numerous other physical and mental problems. There is nothing righteous about it. So, first and foremost, we must accept that *poverty is not a virtue*. Acceptance of that Truth will help us let go of all of the previous programming that has made us feel guilty about attaining prosperity.

The next thing we need to look at is our self-image. Often, the feelings of unworthiness, which we usually take on at a very early age, convince us that we don't deserve to have the good things in life. We usually have difficulty imagining ourselves financially prosperous or imagining ourselves in the most wonderful circumstances possible. Somehow we just don't feel worthy of Limitless Abundance. I want to state emphatically that such belief is a **lie**. It is a misqualification of pure energy. We need to get in touch with those feelings, recognize them for what they are, and let them go. We must begin loving ourselves more, appreciating our uniqueness, recognizing our gifts and talents and accepting that we each have a special skill we can offer this Planet, and the time to start using it is now. We should love ourselves enough to give ourselves what we truly deserve—*the very best.*

We can do a lot more good and help many more people if we have money than we can if we're poor. Money doesn't have to be an instrument of selfishness or greed. Instead, it can be a tool to expand our love and our gifts to the rest of the World. Since we usually use pain as our motivator, it is during our failures and our miserable periods that we develop the incentive to look for a better way and finally become willing to apply the natural Laws of Prosperity. From all outer appearances, I think we are miserable enough. Let's apply the Laws of Prosperity *now* and draw the Limitless Abundance of the Universe into our lives.

Now that we have identified some of the reasons we may have chosen to hold ourselves in a state of financial limitation, we can let go of those concepts of negative thinking and begin developing a Consciousness of Prosperity. Prosperity thinking basically gives us the power to make our dreams come true, whether those dreams are concerned with increased wealth, better health, a happier personal life, more education, career success, a deeper Spiritual life or anything else we desire. We are prosperous to the degree that we are experiencing peace, health and plenty in our Worlds.

Failure is due to failure thinking. **"As a man thinketh in his heart, so he is."** Author James Allen said, *"Through his thoughts, man holds the key to every situation and contains within himself that transforming, regenerative agency by which he may make of himself what he wills."* This is an extremely powerful statement. The laws that govern prosperity are just as sure and workable as the laws that govern mathematics, music, physics and every other field of science.

THE LAW OF THE CIRCLE

We have concluded that every single thing existing in this Universe is composed of electronic Light substance. There are two activities of this electronic substance. One is *radiation*, which means projecting forth or sending out. The other is *magnetization*, which means pulling back or drawing in. Familiar phrases used to describe these two activities are *"giving and receiving," "cause and effect," "action and reaction," "sowing and reaping," "supply and demand"* and *"the inbreath and outbreath"*—in actuality the **Law of the Circle.**

The basic Law of Prosperity is identical. What we radiate out through our thoughts, feelings, mental pictures, words and actions, we magnetize into our lives and affairs. If we are sending out thoughts and feelings of lack and limitation, bogged down with memories of unpleasant, failure experiences and worry or concern over not being able to pay our bills or the fear that we won't have money to purchase our bodily needs, that misqualified energy, charged with the vibration of poverty, is what we will be drawing into our lives and sustaining in our lives.

It is up to us to *dare* to radiate outward through our thoughts, feelings and actions what we *really* want to experience in life rather than dwell on what we're afraid of and what we don't want to experience.

These negative conditions in our lives can change as quickly as we change our thinking about them. We have all heard the expression *"money begets money."* That is true because people who have money have developed true Prosperity Consciousness. They accept prosperity; they feel prosperous; they send out thoughts of prosperity, and they continually draw success and prosperity into their lives.

I know it is a whole lot easier to think and feel and act prosperous when we have money than when we don't, but the important thing is that it is possible, and it is something we *must* learn to do if we are going to attract prosperity into our lives.

Every time we send money out, whether it is to buy groceries, to pay a bill, for entertainment or whatever, we should bless it with gratitude for the service it is providing to us, and let it go freely, knowing that it is a source of energy and, like all energy, it will go out, expand and return to us for more service. If we send our money forth grudgingly, bemoaning the high cost of living, fearing we won't have enough to cover our expenses, hating to spend it on the necessities of life, we will automatically block the flow of the Universe from pouring into our lives. Now, this does not mean going out and charging things and spending money we don't have, but it does mean recognizing money as a *source of energy* that is providing a service to us that we should accept with gratitude and appreciation.

It is important for us to take our attention off poverty and be deliberate about wealth. Our thoughtforms are magnetic. Through persistence, confidence and acceptance, we can draw the Universal supply of all good things into our lives. Through the steps of creative visualization, we can set our goal of prosperity and begin developing true Prosperity Consciousness.

Imagine that you just won a million-dollar lottery. Feel the elation and buoyancy of prosperity. Experience the feeling of success. Now, visualize all the things you would do with that money. Visualize yourself going to the bank and depositing your check. See yourself joyously paying off all your debts, and absorb that feeling of *freedom.*

Visualize yourself now buying the things you have wanted and needed. See yourself helping friends and loved ones who need assistance. Visualize yourself now as you invest your money wisely so that it will grow and expand and continue to serve you. See yourself contributing generous amounts of money to charities, organizations and causes that you want to support that are improving life on Earth.

Experience happiness and the sense of fulfillment as you use your money, not only to add to the joy of your own life, but to improve life for others on the Planet as well.

Even though you may not win a million-dollar lottery, it is the *feeling* of success and abundance that you **must** generate in order to create a magnetic forcefield to draw prosperity into your life. Hold on to that feeling of buoyancy and joy, and feel that prosperity continually throughout the day. Don't give power to the outer-world appearances by dwelling on lack and limitation. Handle the situations in your life as an objective observer, knowing always that regardless of what is occurring at this moment in your life, the supply of the Universe is limitless, and abundance is on its way to you.

AFFIRM DAILY...

I AM Prosperity.

I let go of the misconception that anyone or anything can withhold from me all that this abundant Universe has for me now.

I AM an open door, and all kinds of riches flow to me now.

I AM an irresistible magnet with the power to draw to myself the supply of all good things according to the thoughts, feelings and mental pictures I continually hold in my consciousness.

I realize that I AM responsible for my life situation, and I have the power to create whatever I wish in my life. As of this moment, I choose to create for myself a life of health, success, happiness and prosperity.

I know that this Universe is filled with God's Abundance, and I accept these riches into my life now. I choose Limitless Abundance for myself and for all Humanity.

I know all of my needs will be perfectly met at all times.

Rapid changes come in all aspects of my life as I now open my mind to the unlimited resources of this Universe.

All of my financial affairs are now in perfect order.

I love doing my work, and I AM richly rewarded, both creatively and financially.

I give my love, my gifts, my all, and I AM therefore rich, well and happy now.

I AM PROSPERITY

THE KEY TO FINANCIAL FREEDOM

Now I want to share with you another very important factor in attaining financial freedom. As I have stated, the two-fold activity of the Universe is radiation and magnetization, give-and-take. When working with Natural Law, there must always be a balance. For every cause, there is an effect, and for every action, there must be a reaction. The Universe has given us our gift of life, the electronic Light Substance that beats our physical hearts and allows us to think, move, breathe and live in the physical plane. In addition to that, the Universe has provided everything we need to survive on Earth. We have the Sun, water, air, food and material for clothing and shelter. We have chosen to live in a society, so we use money to purchase our bodily needs at the present time, **but even without money, the Universe has already provided everything we need to exist on this Planet.**

This is our gift of life, and we have accepted it, used it and benefited from it. *Now we must give something back to the Universe in return for our gift of life.* This is the natural give-and-take of the Universe; when we comply with this Law, we open ourselves up to Limitless Abundance.

What is happening at the present time is that we are spending our money on the basics that the Universe has already provided for free, such as food, water, clothing, shelter, etc. In order to activate the *Limitless flow of Abundance*, we must not just give money back to the Universe to pay for the things that have already been given to us for free. If we simply give money to pay for the services that the Universe has already provided, it is like not giving back anything at all. Consequently, we hold ourselves in a pattern of lack and limitation and only draw to ourselves the *minimum* we need to survive.

The **key to financial freedom** is to give back to the Universe, in loving gratitude, more energy or money than we spend on our bodily needs. This does not mean just spending more money on things we want or enjoy, but rather, it means *giving money back to the Universe in gratitude and appreciation for our gift of life.* In just writing this statement I can already feel the resistance and hear the laments, *"I don't even have money to cover my bills. How do you expect me to give money away?"*

That is just the old entity "fear" cropping up. Just for a moment set it aside, and read the following information with an open mind. The application of this Natural Law is the **key** to your financial freedom.

I will state again: the Natural Law of the Universe is give-and-take. The Universe has given and we have taken. The Universe has given us life, and we have accepted it in the form of electronic energy, Light, air, water, food, clothing and shelter. Now, being subject to Natural Law, we **must** give something back to the Universe. The fact that we have accepted this gift of life from the Universe and have chosen to be in a physical body means that, on a higher level, through our super-conscious minds, we understand about this Law of give-and-take, and we have agreed to it. If we had refused to accept this gift of life, knowing that we were going to have to give something back in return for it, we simply would not have been allowed to come into the physical plane. Obviously, we are here, so we agreed to accept this gift. In other words, *"we have danced to the music, and now it's time to pay the fiddler."*

Throughout history, world religions have been trying to get this fact across to us by having us "tithe," which means giving a tenth of our income to the church. In my personal experience, the reasons for tithing were never explained clearly enough, and there was always so much pressure from the head of the church that it never seemed like a free-will gift, given in loving gratitude, but rather just another bill we had to pay. Because of that attitude, tithing usually doesn't have the effect of opening the prosperity flow. The attitude, motive and Spirit with which we give this money back to the Universe is the most important thing about our gift. Our motivation *must* be that *the money we are giving away is a gift of love we are giving back to the Universe in gratitude and appreciation for our gift of life.*

It is certainly true that we can give all kinds of things back to the Universe to repay our Spiritual obligation. We can give love, time, service, joy, work, etc. But, *like attracts like*, so if we want to increase the money in our lives, **WE MUST GIVE AWAY MONEY**.

We can give this gift of money or energy back to the Universe in a multitude of different ways. Remember, there's no mocking Natural Law, so this gift must always work for the betterment of the Planet with absolutely no strings attached. If we give this money to our children so that it won't be too far away from us, and it will still be in the family, that doesn't count. If we give it to someone to manipulate them and to make them feel obligated to us, that doesn't count. If we give it to the dealers in Las Vegas or for any other gambling activity that we're expecting to win a bundle on, that doesn't count. We must give the money away expecting nothing in return from the person, place, condition or thing we give it to. But the wonderful thing about this gift is that money is energy, and, when we send energy out in this way, it expands and returns to us greatly magnified over what we originally sent out. Even though we expect nothing in return from the person, place, condition or thing we give our money to, we *do* expect something in return from the Universe.

The general rule that has been applied throughout time is that if we will give as little as *ten percent* of our wealth back to the Universe in gratitude for our gift of life, we will have such a flow of abundance in our lives that we won't be able to handle it all. This *ten percent* is not part of our cost of living; it is a love offering for our gift of life.

If we stop and think for a moment, we give waiters and waitresses a twenty percent gratuity. Is it too much to ask to give ten percent for our gift of life?

Whom we choose to give our money to should be our decision. We should not allow ourselves to be pressured into giving our money to people or organizations we don't fully support. That interferes with our ability to believe this is our gift to the Universe, and it blocks our flow.

Our money can be given to Spiritual institutions, organizations that we feel are teaching people how to improve the quality of their lives, scientific research, universities and learning institutions, organizations for music and the arts, charities, needy families, environmental protection organizations, animal rights organizations, human rights organizations or any other constructive activity that we would like to support.

For those of you who are still experiencing resistance and feeling *"there is no way I can possibly af ford to do that,"* please understand that **you don't have any choice in the matter**. You have already accepted your gift of life, and now you **must** give something back to the Universe *in one way or another*. It is Natural Law.

Unfortunately, because of our lack of understanding about this Law, the large majority of people are giving this energy back through drudgery and suffering and the sweat of their brows, working long, difficult hours for a meager existence. This agony is one way of giving energy back to the Universe, but it is certainly not the best way or the most enjoyable way, and by no means is it the most constructive way. Even though we may have made this choice to remain in a state of drudgery at a subconscious level, it was still our own free-will choice. Consequently, we have the absolute free will to change our method of repayment to the Universe.

In order to open the flow of Limitless Abundance into our lives, we must freely give money back to the Universe for things other than just covering the expenses of our bodily needs. The most painless way, and the most profitable way, is a method I'll refer to as *seed money*. Seed money is money we deliberately give back to the Universe, knowing that it will expand at least ten-fold on its return to us. This is money we give away to any activity, organization, institution or person of our choice, with no strings attached, expecting nothing in return from them but accepting that the Natural Law of the Universe will expand that money at least ten-fold on its return to us. It's important that we understand clearly that we don't expect anything from the recipient of our money, but we *do* expect the Flow of Abundance from the Universal Source of all Life...God.

To activate this Flow of Abundance, we need to consciously put our attention on it with our thoughts, words, feelings and actions. We need to know and accept that this is a Scientific Law. As we give our money away in loving gratitude for our gift of life, *we must consciously claim our ten-fold return.* As an example, if we give $100 away, we must consciously say, ***"I AM receiving $1,000 from the Limitless Flow of God's Abundance, with the highest good of all concerned,"*** accepting beyond a shadow of a doubt that the money is on its way back to us. When we say *"with the highest good of all concerned,"* we eliminate the possibility of negative interference. We must never be willing to attain prosperity at the expense of anyone else. This will tragically backfire in our faces. I know from outer appearances it seems as though many people have attained great wealth by being dishonest and stepping on people along the way. But I assure you, we cannot take anything away from someone else without something being taken away from us. We have often heard that people spend the first forty years of their lives acquiring their fortunes and the next forty years spending their fortunes trying to regain their health. That is a graphic example of the accuracy of the Law when the wealth is acquired by unethical means.

After we have claimed our ten-fold return, we must feel gratitude for that gift. Gratitude opens the door to God's Abundance, and it's an indispensable catalyst for our ten-fold return.

It is imperative that we not worry about where the money will be coming from. By putting our attention and concern into where the money could possibly come from, we actually limit ourselves and set up blocks. We must just accept, believe, know and feel that the money is flowing back to us in accordance with Natural Law.

Our return can come from totally unexpected sources. Just remember, that with seed money, the ten-fold return *is expected*; the means of that return *is unexpected*. Through the proper application of this Law, our prosperity is assured and can be limited only by our lack of consistency. The supply of the Universe is limitless, and its flow into our lives has been blocked only by our own misapplication of the Law.

If you are currently having trouble making ends meet, I know it is difficult to even think of giving away ten percent of your income, but, if you are going to get out of that situation, you have to begin somewhere. If you can really accept that for every $10 you give away, you will receive $100 in return, *which is the Truth of the Law,* then it will make it easier to let go. You can begin by giving away $5 or $10 here and there, claiming your ten-fold return each time. Then, with courage, give away more and more until you begin to experience the wonderful Flow of Prosperity.

There are a few questions that always come up on this subject, so I will answer them now. One question is, *"If I don't have any money to give away, can I give away my services or my time or something else?"* It is certainly better to give away something rather than nothing, but remember, the Law is *like attracts like.* So if you want to attract **money** into your life, you need to give **money** away. Do the best you can. As soon as you can start giving money away, do it, even if you start with only a dollar.

Another question is, *"Does it count if I claim this gift as a deduction on my income tax?"* There is nothing wrong with claiming this deduction on your income tax as long as that was not your reason for giving the gift. If you did it *only* for a tax writeoff, then, of course, it doesn't count as a love offering for your gift of life.

Another question is, *"I feel guilty giving this money*

as a gift of love and then expecting a ten-fold return. Are you sure this is fair?" This is not only fair, it is part of our gift of life that we have been refusing to accept, actually rejecting. These feelings of guilt stem from our old programming of believing that somehow it is Spiritual to be poor, or that it's not "right" to want money. We keep hearing the statement, *"Money is the root of all evil."* That is not what the Bible says at all. The statement is *"The **worship** of money is the root of all evil,"* which is quite a different matter.

And the last question people ask is, *"Do I give away ten percent of my gross or ten percent of my net income?"* Of course the answer to that question is...it depends if you want a ten-fold return of your gross or your net income.

DIVINE INTERVENTION

In addition to tithing, in order for us to eliminate poverty in our lives, we must fully participate in another activity of Light. We must release and transmute all of the etheric records and memories of the past that vibrate at any level of poverty consciousness. We must then create a new etheric blueprint of Prosperity Consciousness and reprogram that blueprint into every level of our minds, feelings, actions and beliefs.

Because of the urgency of the hour and the criticalness of this moment on Earth, God and the Legions of Light Who abide in the Heavenly Realms to do His or Her Will, have evaluated Humanity's greatest need. It has been determined that even the illumined souls have too far to go to truly eliminate poverty in their lives through the natural progression of evolution in time to turn things around before it is too late. Consequently, it has been decreed by Cosmic Law that **Divine Intervention is necessary.**

The Light on the Planet has been expanding daily and hourly for several years. Through the unified efforts of millions of Awakened Light Beings on Earth who have joined together in consciousness for Global meditations of World Peace and Planetary Healing, a Planetary security system, which expands from Heart Center to Heart Center among the Light Beings, has been anchored deep into the Earth's Crystal Grid System. This has caused the vibratory rate of the Planet to increase. Whenever large numbers of souls volunteer to selflessly expand the Light of the World, special Cosmic Dispensations are granted and additional amounts of Light from the Heart of God are released to balance Humanity's efforts. The additional allotment of energy is always released into the World in a way that will fulfill Humanity's greatest need. It has been determined by the Godhead that the greatest need of the hour is THE ELIMINATION OF POVERTY AND THE ACTIVATION OF THE FLOW OF ABUNDANCE INTO THE LIVES OF THE AWAKENED LIGHT BEINGS ON EARTH.

The illumined souls who are truly striving to improve the quality of life on the Planet often consider poverty to be a virtue. This is creating a very difficult challenge. With the increased influx of Light, the illumined souls are awakening. They are learning to reach into the Divine Mind of God to tap the Wisdom that will reveal viable solutions to the World's woes. But they do not have the financial sustenance to bring these glorious ideas into physical reality.

As we awaken, we begin to perceive the magnitude of our purpose and reason for Being. As the Divine Ideas from the Mind of God flow into our consciousness, we are recognizing ways and means of developing tangible alternatives to our present course of action which appears to be planetary destruction. The ideas are wonderful and resonate with mutual respect for all life on Earth.   There are ideas for alternative energy and fuel systems that will not pollute the air or use up our limited resources; ideas for alternative plans for food production that will feed the entire Planet; ideas for alternative economic systems that will bring prosperity and abundance to all Humanity; ideas for alternative health systems that will allow each person access to the optimum treatment for their particular affliction; ideas for alternative ways of disposing of and recycling our excess so that our Beloved Earth will flourish, and there are limitless other ideas for alternatives that will transform this Planet into Freedom's Holy Star.

It is time for us to recognize and accept that we live in the physical plane of existence, and we must deal with this physical reality.   That means if we are going to bring the new, innovative ideas into physical manifestation, we must utilize the existing means of exchange, which at the present time is money.   It is time for the Awakening Light Beings of the World to open up to the limitless flow of God's Abundance, so we can have the necessary money to accomplish the magnificent goals and ideas pouring into our consciousness from the Realms of Illumined Truth.   It is time to bring these ideas into physical reality.

In order to help us accomplish this, we are being given superhuman assistance.   The entire Company of Heaven is joining forces in this endeavor, and the opportunity being presented to us to achieve PERMANENT FINANCIAL FREEDOM is unprecedented. We must remember, however, that not even God will interfere with our gift of Free Will.   In order for us to fully benefit from this unparalleled opportunity, we must take the necessary action and choose, on a conscious level, to release and transmute all past accep-

24

tance of poverty—cause, core, effect, record and memory. We must also transmute, through the Power of Forgiveness, all we have ever done to abuse the substance of money, all we have ever done to manipulate, dominate, control or hurt any part of life through selfishness, greed or the misuse of money. We must also forgive all those who, in any way, used the substance of money to abuse us. We must literally go back in consciousness, through the Ages of time, and ask God to transmute every electron of precious life energy we have ever misqualified in relation to money. This must penetrate into every existence and dimension we have ever experienced, both known and unknown, piercing deep into every electron we have ever released that is vibrating at a frequency less than absolute Abundance, Prosperity, Opulence, the God Supply of all Good Things and Financial Freedom.

In order for us to accomplish this incredible feat in the time allotted, we are receiving Divine Intervention. The most intensified activity of the Law of Forgiveness ever manifest in the history of time is being released into the atmosphere of Earth. This Violet Light is pouring forth from the very Heart of God, and It is vibrating at frequencies of the Fifth Dimension. These are frequencies of perfection that we have never before been able to withstand on Earth.

Since the shift of vibration that took place on the Planet during Harmonic Convergence (August 15-17, 1987), the vibratory rate of Earth has been increasing daily and hourly the maximum that we can withstand. We are now capable of withstanding more Light than ever before. It is crucial that we clearly understand, that even though this glorious Light of Forgiveness is available for us to use to transmute our past actions and beliefs which are anchored in poverty consciousness, the only way we will experience the effect of this gift tangibly in our everyday lives is to draw it through our Heart Flames and consciously project it into the physical plane. It has always been said *"God needs a body."* The Law is that in order for something to manifest in the physical plane, it must be drawn through the Divine Spark pulsating in the heart of someone abiding in the physical plane. That simply means that, even though this splendid gift is pouring into the atmosphere of Earth, if we don't invoke it into our lives and project it into our life experiences through our thoughts, words, actions and feelings, we will not receive its benefits or create lives of permanent financial freedom for ourselves.

Fortunately, the entire Company of Heaven, always functioning under the auspices of Divine Order, never releases such a gift to the finite minds of Humanity without releasing the wisdom and understanding of how to effectively utilize such a precious gift. We have been given a guided visualization and an Activity of Light by the Realms of Illumined Truth that will enable each and every one of us to take advantage of this momentous opportunity.

Utilizing the Violet Light of Forgiveness is the first step of a two-fold Activity of Light that is necessary to eliminate poverty in our lives. The second step involves creating a new etheric blueprint of Prosperity Consciousness and integrating that Divine Pattern into every level of our minds, feelings, actions and beliefs.

The time is so very short before we must reclaim our Divine Heritage and again manifest Heaven on Earth as decreed through the Lord's Prayer, *"Thy Kingdom come, Thy Will be done on Earth as it is in Heaven."* A Clarion Call is reverberating throughout the Universe invoking assistance for the Earth. The response is coming from myriad Legions of Illumined

Beings. These glorious Beings of Light are descending into the atmosphere of Earth. They are magnetizing the Eternal Light of God that is always Victorious into the Earth. As One Unified Presence, One Holy Breath, One Heartbeat, One Thought, One Energy and Vibration, One Consciousness of pure God Light, these Divine Beings are creating a Cosmic Forcefield in the atmosphere of Earth that has the capability of transforming the distorted experience of poverty back into the original Divine Plan. That Plan is for the continual flow of God's Abundance to pour into the everyday lives of all lifestreams evolving on Earth. The Cosmic Forcefield has the power to change our Earthly experience at an atomic, cellular level and will shift our vibratory rate into a new etheric blueprint of prosperity. This Sacred Gift is available to all who choose to lift up in consciousness and magnetize Its Holy Essence into the physical plane of Earth. We have been given a guided visualization that will assist each of us to do just that.

The wonderful thing about the Divine Intervention taking place on Earth is that we don't have to fully understand it. We don't have to believe it; we don't even have to accept it. All we have to do to benefit from it is ask, through the Presence of God anchored in our hearts, that it flow into our lives. The Law is *"Ask and you shall receive; knock and the door will be opened."* If you will trust enough to ask God to allow these Divine Gifts to flow into your life, on the return current of that very plea, you will begin to experience the frequencies of prosperity.

Read this information, or listen to the tapes over and over again. Ask the Presence of God pulsating within you to filter out every trace of human consciousness and accept only the words that resonate as Truth in your own heart. Do the exercises and visualizations daily, and know that each time this information is read or the tapes are played, it adds to the building momentum of Prosperity Consciousness in your own individual life and in the lives of all Humanity as well. Step-by-step your physical reality is changing, and instead of reflecting lack and limitation, you are beginning to reflect the God Supply of all Good Things: Prosperity, Abundance, Opulence and Financial Freedom.

CLAIMING YOUR PROSPERITY

The Divine Gifts from the Realms of Perfection that are being made available to all Humanity during this Cosmic Moment of planetary transformation must be magnetized into the physical plane of Earth through **our God Selves** and not through our lower human egos.

Our lower human egos are composed of a synthesis of all the activities we have expressed through our physical, etheric, mental and emotional bodies during our Earthly sojourns. This part of our identity was created gradually as we experienced life through our limited, physical senses. Much of the poverty Humanity has experienced is because we have perceived the lower human ego to be an intelligence apart from God. We have given it power and dominion by accepting and believing that this limited, struggling self is who we really are. We lost the awareness of our true God Selves, and as a result, we have bound ourselves in the distorted perception of extreme lack and limitation. As long as we believe we are separate from God, we will experience the painful conditions of poverty. Only when we accept our God Selves will we allow God's Limitless Abundance to flow into our lives. When we actually accept our God Selves *as* ourselves and not some separate *"self"* we occasionally call upon, our lives will reflect an entirely new picture, and instead of poverty, we will create prosperity. We are now being given the opportunity, through Divine Intervention, to pass over the threshold into individual and planetary transformation. Our God Selves are One with the all-encompassing Presence of God, and They continually prod and prompt us ever onward to our highest potential. When we give our God Selves dominion in our lives, we are lifted into octaves of awareness and understanding that enable us to clearly KNOW *"all that the Father-Mother God has is mine."* We recognize that prosperity is our natural state of Being, and abundance is available in every aspect of our lives now.

As we harmoniously focus our attention on the perfection of our true God Selves, our lower human personalities are lifted up and integrated into those radiant Presences of Light. Then we are able to function on Earth as the Children of God we truly are.

We accomplish this integration by going within and re-establishing a loving relationship with our God Selves. When we do this, we begin to recognize and accept our God Selves. Then an awakening takes place, and we begin to activate, within our consciousness, the deep memory that has always known of our Divinity. From this level of consciousness, we know through every fiber of our Beings, *I AM Limitless Prosperity; I AM the continual Flow of God's Abundance.* We understand that the Presence of God always pulsates within our hearts, and It is all-knowing, all-caring, all-loving and all-powerful.

When we reunite with our God Presences, Divine energy flows in and through us. This Divine energy is the fulfillment of every good and perfect thing. It is completely impersonal, and when It flows through our newly-developed Forcefield of God Consciousness, It has no choice but to manifest perfection here and now. Prosperity is then reclaimed as our natural state of Being.

Now it is time for each of us to utilize the full power of our Divinity, our God Self, to invoke into our lives the full-gathered momentum of the sacred gift of the Violet Light of Forgiveness—the gift which is pouring forth into the atmosphere of Earth from the very Heart of God—the gift which is being given to Humanity at this Cosmic Moment to transmute all frequencies of poverty consciousness—the gift which represents the greatest influx of the Law of Forgiveness ever manifested in the history of time.

After we invoke the Violet Light of Forgiveness together as One Unified Consciousness, we will join with the entire Company of Heaven and magnetize the Cosmic Forcefield of Prosperity that is pulsating in the atmosphere into the everyday lives of all Awakened Light Beings evolving on Planet Earth.

TRANSMUTING POVERTY CONSCIOUSNESS

All is in readiness. To participate in this Divine Activity of Light, please sit comfortably in your chair with your arms and legs uncrossed, your spine as straight as possible and your hands resting gently in your lap with your palms facing upward.

Breathe in deeply, and as you exhale, let all of the tension of the day just drop away, and feel yourself becoming completely relaxed. Breathe in deeply again, and as you exhale, feel your God Self take full dominion of your four lower bodies. Your mind is activated. The cobwebs of confusion or doubt or fear are swept away, and you become mentally alert and vibrantly aware. You realize that, through the radiance of your God Presence, you are enveloped in a Forcefield of Invincible Protection which prevents anything that is not of the Light from distracting you or interfering with this sacred moment.

You feel the deep inner glow of peace and well-being. You experience the buoyant joy of expectancy and enthusiasm. You accept that **you are the open door that no one can shut**.

Now please follow me through this visualization with the full power of your attention. I will write in the first person so each of us can experience this Activity of Light tangibly and personally in our own lives.

Beloved Presence of God blazing in my heart...I know and accept that, through this invocation, You have taken command of my four lower bodies. My physical, etheric, mental and emotional bodies are now being raised in vibration, and they are being integrated with Your Radiant Presence. My awareness is increasing, and I begin to perceive clearly Your *"still, small voice within."* I know that You respond to my every call for assistance. I AM beginning to experience Your exquisite vibrations, and my entire Being is flooded with Light. My consciousness is opening to the influx of Your pure, Spiritual energy. From this new level of awareness, I now know, as never before, *You are in me, and I AM in Thee. I KNOW You are me.*

I AM a Being of Radiant Light!
I AM One with the energy and vibration
that is the all-encompassing Presence of God.
I AM One with the Divine Love
that fills the Universe with the glory of Itself.
I AM One with every particle of life.
I AM One with the Divine Plan for Planet Earth.
I AM One with the Limitless Flow

of God's Abundance.
I AM that I AM.

A reactivation and initiation into multidimensional awareness is occurring within me.

I AM lifted up, closer in vibration to the very Heart of God. The pre-encoded memories that were implanted deep within my cellular patterns aeons ago are activated. These patterns reveal my Divine Plan, my purpose and reason for Being. I AM experiencing a great soaring and awakening as I remember my Divine Heritage.

I AM stepping through the doorway into multidimensional Reality. Here I AM empowered with even more rarified frequencies of Divinity. Moment-to-moment, this radiant Light is awakening within me previously untapped levels of wisdom and illumination. I easily grasp each Divine thought and idea. As I do, avenues of opportunity unfold before me. I feel a sense of elation as each opportunity presents itself. I joyously seize the Divine Opportunities, and I feel a greater sense of self-worth and accomplishment than ever before. My life is pulsating with a sense of meaning and warmth.

I AM now lifted higher into the Realms of Perfection...and now higher...and now higher.

In this Realm, I easily release and let go of attachments and behavior patterns that do not support my highest good. I release all patterns that reflect a consciousness less than prosperity. I recognize *this is the moment of my new beginning.*

I now have the absolute ability to Create Prosperity Consciousness, and I do so easily and joyously.

I AM experiencing my true integrity.
I AM trustworthy and honest.
I AM an expression of Divine Truth.
I AM worthy and deserving of prosperity, and
I AM able to transform every aspect of my life now.

Change is manifesting through Divine Grace and Love. As each aspect of my life that needs changing surfaces before me, I easily love it free and forgive myself for my perceived transgression.

I know I AM a child of God, and I deserve to be loved and forgiven. As the changes take place, I AM experiencing a sense of inner calm, patience and silence.

I AM in the Divine flow of my true God Reality. I AM One with the Infinite Intelligence within me, and I AM *always* able to make correct choices. I love myself unconditionally, and I AM grateful for this opportunity to change, which I accept with deep humility.

The Divine Power to sustain these changes is continually flowing through me, and from this moment forth, I choose to create a life of prosperity and only that which supports my highest good.

Once again I AM lifted higher into the Realms of Perfection...and now higher...and now higher.

I now focus on the Sacred Essence of my Holy Breath.

I realize that with every *inbreath* I extend in consciousness, through my eternal journey into Infinity, to the Source of never-ending perfection. With every *outbreath*, I magnetize the full momentum of that perfection and radiate its full blessing to all life evolving on Earth.

My inbreath is the open portal to the Pure Land of Boundless Splendor and Infinite Light, and my outbreath is the source of all Divine Blessings for Humanity and the Planet. I understand now that the Divine Gifts being presented to Humanity from the Legions of Light serving this sweet Earth will be drawn into the world of form on the Holy Breath.

I consecrate and dedicate myself to be the open door for these sacred Gifts of Light.

Lord, make me an instrument of Your Limitless Abundance. I AM the Flaming Hand of God, now made manifest in the physical plane of Earth.

I AM now ready, through every level of my consciousness, to release, let go of and transmute every frequency of vibration, every single electron of precious life energy I have ever released in any existence or dimension that is expressing a pattern less than God's Limitless Flow of Abundance, Prosperity, Opulence, the Supply of all Good Things and Financial Freedom.

I AM enveloped in an Invincible Forcefield of Protection and Eternal Peace. I AM able to review my life as an objective observer. I ask my God Self to push to the surface of my conscious mind every experience I have ever had, both known and unknown, that is in any way preventing me from attaining prosperity. As these experiences begin to surface, I breathe in deeply. On the Holy Breath, I pierce into the gift of the Violet Light of Forgiveness. I absorb the most powerful Gift of Forgiveness ever manifest in the history of time, and I breathe it in, through and around my four lower vehicles and all of the energy surfacing and returning to me now to be loved free. This sacred Violet Light from the very Heart of God instantly transmutes the negative thoughts, words, actions, feelings, beliefs and memories that are blocking my eternal financial freedom. Every electron of energy is being transformed back into its original perfection.

My God Self now expands this Activity of Light and reaches back into the Ages of time to magnetize every electron of energy stamped with my individual electronic pattern into the gift of the Violet Light of Forgiveness. These records and memories surface effortlessly, and I AM able to let them go without pain or fear. I feel the buoyant joy of freedom.

I continue breathing in as I reach deeper into the sacred gift of Violet Light, and I exhale Its Divine Essence to flood the physical plane of Earth.

I affirm with deep feeling and a true inner knowing...

I AM a force of the Violet Light of Forgiveness,
greater than anything less than prosperity.

I now realize I AM able to transmute, through the power of this sacred gift, the mass consciousness of poverty. All records and memories of Humanity's abuse of the substance of money flow into the Violet Light of Forgiveness.

Under the direction of my God Self and the entire Company of Heaven, every electron of poverty consciousness that has ever been released by any part of life, in any existence or dimension, both known and unknown, is surfacing for transmutation by the Violet Light of Forgiveness.

The transformation is taking place as each electron enters the Violet Light and is instantly transmuted—

cause, core, effect, record and memory—back into the frequencies of prosperity and God's Limitless Abundance.

I AM a force of the Violet Light of Forgiveness,
greater than anything less than prosperity.

I AM a force of the Violet Light of Forgiveness,
greater than anything less than prosperity.

I AM a force of the Violet Light of Forgiveness,
greater than anything less than prosperity.

I AM Free!   I AM Free!   I AM Free!
I AM Eternally Financially Free!
It is done!   And, So It Is!

I ask, through the Presence of God pulsating in my heart, that this sacred Activity of Light be maintained, eternally self-sustained, increased with my every breath, daily and hourly, moment-to-moment, the maximum that Cosmic Law will allow, until all life belonging to or serving the Earth at this time is wholly Ascended and Free.

THE DIVINE GIFT OF PROSPERITY

I AM now lifted up in consciousness even higher into the Realms of Perfection...and now higher...and now higher.

I pass over the Highway of Light that bridges Heaven and Earth. I enter the Pure Land of Boundless Splendor and Infinite Light that radiates in the atmosphere of Earth, and *I KNOW I AM ONE WITH GOD.*

All the Light Beings evolving on Earth are joining me in consciousness in this Octave of Pure Joy. I know I AM One with every part of life. As one unified voice, we send forth the Clarion Call into the Universe invoking our illumined brothers and sisters to come and help us in our moment of transformation. The Cosmic Tone of our unified voice reverberates through all dimensions, and the response comes from every corner of the Cosmos.

I see the luminous Presence of Legions of Divine Beings descending into the atmosphere of Earth. They take Their strategic positions above me and begin forming a tremendous circle as They stand shoulder-to-shoulder.

As One Unified Consciousness, One Holy Breath, One Heartbeat, One Energy and Vibration of Perfection, They breathe into Their Heart Flames the **Golden Ray of Eternal Peace and Opulence** from the very Heart of God. This resplendent Golden Light contains within Its Holy Vibration every frequency of God's Abundance. It is the most glorious, scintillating color of gold I have ever seen. As these magnificent Beings absorb the essence of Opulence into Their Heart Flames, They become blazing Golden Suns of Light. They now, in perfect synchronicity, breathe the Golden Light into the center of the circle. As the Golden Rays of Light pour forth from Their Heart Centers into the center of the circle, the Rays begin to merge, forming a brilliant Golden Sun. This Sun is the matrix within which the Cosmic Forcefield of Prosperity Consciousness will form.

The Beings of Light now magnetize the thoughtform of the Forcefield of Prosperity which is held in the Divine Mind of God. The blueprint forms within the Golden Sun. It is a radiant, scintillating Golden Pyramid of Light, and pulsating within Its base is a shimmering Golden Lotus Blossom. With each pulsation of the Lotus Blossom, concentric circles of Divine Opulence are projected into the physical plane of Earth to bathe every particle of life evolving here in the glory of God's Abundance. Unformed primal Light substance is now magnetized into the etheric blueprint, and the Golden Pyramid of Opulence is tangibly manifest. Its resplendent beauty pulsates continually in the atmosphere of Earth, to be sustained through the unified efforts of the entire Company of Heaven until all life evolving here is wholly Ascended and Free.

Now, the Light Beings on Earth prepare to be the open portals through which this Divine Gift of Prosperity will manifest in the world of form.

The Flame of Divinity, blazing in every human heart, begins expanding to envelop the four lower bodies of each Awakened Light Being. I experience a beautiful Blue Flame blazing through my left brain hemisphere and the left side of my body. This is the Masculine Polarity of God qualified with Divine Will and Power. I experience a beautiful Pink Flame blazing through my right brain hemisphere and the right side of my body. This is the Feminine Polarity of God qualified with Divine Love. As the Masculine and Feminine Polarities of God are balanced within me, I experience rising up between them the Sunshine Yellow Flame of God which is qualified with Divine Wisdom and Illumination.

I AM now enveloped in the Victorious Three-fold Flame, and I AM the expression of my true God Self!

From this consciousness of Divinity, I magnetize into my Heart Center a Golden Ray of Light from the tremendous Pyramid of Prosperity pulsating above me.

As the Ray of Light merges with the Spark of Divinity in my heart, a miniature replica of the Golden Pyramid with the Golden Lotus Blossom is formed. This creates a magnetic forcefield in my heart that enables me to draw the full momentum of blessings from this sacred Pyramid into my everyday life experience.

I breathe in deeply, and as I do, I pierce into the Golden Pyramid of Light. I absorb the Golden Light of Opulence pulsating from the Lotus Blossom, and as I exhale, a cascading fountain of Golden Light pours through my Heart Center into the physical plane of Earth. This sacred Light of God's Abundance floods the Planet and flows into the hands of every Light Being, every Activity of Light, every conscious person who will, in any way, shape or form, use this Gift of Prosperity to improve the quality of life on Earth. Through this gift, the substance of money becomes tangibly available and flows continually into the hands and use of every lifestream, organization or activity that is receiving the ideas from the Divine Mind of God to restore this Planet to Her Divine Heritage which is Heaven on Earth. The money flows easily and effortlessly into the tangible use of all on the Planet who are operating from a consciousness of Reverence for ALL Life.

As the Golden Light of Prosperity reaches Its furthest destination in the world of form, flooding every particle of life with financial sustenance, It begins Its return journey back to the Source. First It flows back to my Heart Flame, which sent It forth. As this Sacred Light flows back into my heart, It brings with It the Limitless Flow of Money and the God Supply of all Good Things.

My life now reflects the
Gift of Permanent Financial Freedom.

*From this moment forth, everything I need to fulfill
my Divine Plan is always available to me.*

*The Divine Law of **"Ask and you shall receive"**
is instantly manifest.*

*I feel the buoyancy and elation of my newfound
freedom, and the entire Company of Heaven
rejoices with me as I reclaim my
Divine Birthright of Abundance
through Prosperity Consciousness.*

*I AM! I AM! I AM!...

*The eternally sustained manifestation of God's Lim-
itless Supply of Money and every Good Thing I require
to assist me in my service to the Light, now made manifest and sustained by Holy Grace. (Repeat three times
from *)*

It is done! And, So It Is!

I now breathe in deeply and return my consciousness to the room. I become aware of my physical body
and gently move my hands and feet.

I AM aware that I AM a multidimensional Being,
and I abide at once in both the Pure Land of Boundless
Splendor and Infinite Light and the physical world of
form on Earth.

With my every breath I AM continually an open
portal for the full magnitude of the Sacred Gifts of Prosperity to pour into the everyday lives of all the Awak-

ened Light Beings and all Activities of Light on the Planet.

I realize that each time I read this information, play the Prosperity tapes or consciously energize the thoughtform, the sacred Gifts of Prosperity will build in momentum and effectiveness. Moment-by-moment the transformation will occur, and the new etheric blueprint of Abundance for all Life embraced within the Divine Understanding of Reverence, Mutual Respect and a Higher Consciousness of always seeking the Highest Good for all concerned will become the **Order of the New Cosmic Day**.

THANK YOU, GOD!!!

BOOK ORDER FORM

IT IS TIME FOR YOU
TO BE FINANCIALLY FREE!

Please send me _____ copy(ies) of the book *It is Time for YOU to be Financially Free* at $7.00 each plus postage/handling.

POSTAGE/HANDLING

Up to $20.00..... $ 5.00	*For all Canada & Mexico orders, please add an additional 6% of the **subtotal**. For all other foreign countries, please add an additional 8% of the **subtotal**. *For all foreign orders, please make payment by Visa, MasterCard or International **Postal** Money Order. No checks, please.*
$20.01-$36.00.... 6.00	
$36.01-$50.00.... 7.00	
$50.01-$75.00.... 9.00	
$75.01-$90.00.... 10.00	
$90.01 & over.... 11.00	

Book   Subtotal $_____
Postage $_____
*Additional postage
for foreign mailing $_____
Total $_____

Name_____

Address_____

City_____ State_____ Zip _____

Country_____ Phone _____

If paying by credit card, please complete the following:
VISA ☐ MASTERCARD ☐

Name on card_____ _____

Card Number_____ __ _____

Exp. Date_____   Amount $_____

Mail to: The New Age Study of Humanity's Purpose, PO Box 41883, Tucson AZ 85717, Phone 520-885-7909, Fax 520-751-3835

CASSETTE TAPE ORDER FORM

PROSPERITY TAPES

Please send me:

_____ tape(s) of **The Key to Financial Freedom** at $9.00 each plus postage/handling.

_____ tape(s) of **The Gift to Reclaim Your Prosperity** at $9.00 each plus postage/handling.

POSTAGE/HANDLING

Up to $20.00..... $ 5.00	*For all Canada & Mexico orders, please add an additional 6% of the **subtotal**. For all other foreign countries, please add an additional 8% of the **subtotal**. For all foreign orders, please make payment by Visa, MasterCard or International **Postal** Money Order. No checks, please.
$20.01-$36.00.... 6.00	
$36.01-$50.00.... 7.00	
$50.01-$75.00.... 9.00	
$75.01-$90.00.... 10.00	
$90.01 & over.... 11.00	

Tape   Subtotal $_____
Postage $_____
*Additional postage
for foreign mailing $_____
Total $_____

Name_____

Address_____

City_____ State_____ Zip _____

Country_____ Phone _____

If paying by credit card, please complete the following:
                    VISA ☐ MASTERCARD ☐

Name on card_____

Card Number_____

Exp. Date_____   Amount $_____

Mail to: The New Age Study of Humanity's Purpose, PO Box 41883, Tucson AZ 85717, Phone 520-885-7909, Fax 520-751-3835

```
┌─────────────────────────┐
│      NEWSLETTER          │
└─────────────────────────┘
```

TAKE CHARGE OF YOUR LIFE

**NEVER BEFORE HAVE WE BEEN
AS BLESSED WITH SACRED KNOWLEDGE
AS WE ARE DURING THIS UNIQUE TIME
WHEN THE REALMS OF TRUTH
HAVE PIERCED THROUGH THE VEIL
TO MEET US HALFWAY**

This newsletter is a timely, **monthly publication** that shares information on the unprecedented Activities of Light now taking place on Earth. These activities involve the unfolding Divine Plan that is now ushering in the reality of Heaven on Earth.

Take Charge of Your Life includes information that is pouring forth from the Realms of Illumined Truth and guidance from the Spiritual Hierarchy that will assist all Humanity during these wondrous but challenging times. It contains words of encouragement that will lift you up and fill your heart with hope and joy.

The subscription rate is $36.00 per year for USA. For Canada and Mexico, the rate is $42.00 per year. For all other foreign countries, the rate is $46.00 per year.

*ORDER FORM FOR
TAKE CHARGE OF YOUR LIFE NEWSLETTER
ON PAGE 46*

I would like to subscribe to the monthly newsletter "TAKE CHARGE OF YOUR LIFE." Enclosed is the annual subscription fee of $36.00. For Canada and Mexico please add $6.00 postage. For all other countries please add $10.00. *For all foreign orders, please make payment by Visa, MasterCard or International **Postal** Money Order. No checks, please.*

Please send check or money order to:
The New Age Study of Humanity's Purpose
P.O. Box 41883
Tucson, AZ 85717
Phone 520-885-7909, Fax 520-751-3835

Name_____

Address_____

City_____ State_____ Zip_____

Country_____ Phone_____

If paying be credit card, please complete the following:
Visa ☐   MasterCard ☐

Number_____ Card Exp._____

Name on Card _____

Signature_____

ADDITIONAL OPPORTUNITIES

If you are not on our mailing list and would like to be,
_____ please check here.

Information on available tapes and books from The
_____ New Age Study of Humanity's Purpose.

_____ Sample of our newsletter *Take Charge of Your Life*.

_____ Information on The World Congress On Illumination.

_____ Information on our Free Seminars.

_____ All of the above.

NAME_____

ADDRESS_____

CITY_____

STATE_____ ZIP _____

COUNTRY _____

Please mail to:
    The New Age Study Of Humanity's Purpose
    P.O. Box 41883, Tucson AZ 85717
    or Fax to 520-751-3835

FREE SEMINARS

We have been directed from within the very core of our Beings to create an avenue through which the Divine Knowledge that is now pouring forth from the Realms of Illumined Truth will be freely accessible to the masses. To fulfill this Divine Directive, we decided to offer **FREE SEMINARS** throughout the country.

We began this holy endeavor in December 1993, and conduct seven or eight seminars each year. We average between 300 and 500 people at each seminar. The response from grateful participants is overwhelming. Here are a few of their comments from letters we have received:

"...Thank you for the California seminar. I would not have been able to afford to go to one. It answered so-o-o many questions. I want to share this information now with those who need help."

B. in Los Angeles, California

"...Words cannot express the gratitude I feel for your Presence in the Bay Area. Boy! Did you charge this place up. The seminar was wonderful. To be able to put into five hours my 25 years of Lightwork totally amazed me. It was complete common sense, yet overwhelming...yet a definite awakening. It was beautiful. It was Heaven to be in your Light. Thank you and all the Blessed Staff."

A. in San Francisco, California

"I attended your free seminar in Vancouver, B.C., Canada. I was so deeply moved. All my life I have searched for answers. Listening to you was magical; it all made sense. Like somewhere deep in my very inner soul this was what I had always searched for. I felt a real connection—my lifeforce and purpose was found. I am working through letting go of unworthiness, sadness and guilt. My schizophrenic sister is my greatest teacher.

"Your books and tapes are fabulous. I have connected with "Stargate of the Heart," "The Next Step" and "The Awakening."

50

"Thanks so much for being MY TEACHER. I have changed so much and am gaining newfound confidence. My quest is to share with everyone I meet. Love is the answer. Thank you from the bottom of my heart."
Love,
S. in Abbotsford, B.C, Canada

"The gratitude of the general Sedona Family goes out to you and your Family team. The work you all do in the Enlightenment is much appreciated.

"The seminar in Phoenix was well done, as always, but this time I felt a great empowerment given by the collection of souls who chose to be present. Each person brought with them so many heart and soul gifts that were distributed one to the other and then out into Humanity. Also, the Masters made Themselves known. At one point, a number of Them came in from the edges of the room and crossed in front of you as you spoke.

"When Peaches came up to sing, the field became a steady purple field.

"We thank you for your wisdom speaking; Kay, for powerful meditations that helped create a unified field of Light and Peaches for the Joy she instilled in us all. Thanks again. Love from us all"
God's Blessing,
K. in Rimrock, Arizona

"I heard you speak in San Diego. Never before have I heard words that resonated so much within me. I'm reading "Stargate of the Heart" and listening to "Learning to Love Yourself" in the car as I drive everywhere.

"Thank you so much for doing the work that you do, for spreading the words of the Master."
G. in San Diego, California

"Thank you for your inspiring seminar. You revealed to me what I have always known in my heart. Thank you for reminding us of who we really are."
L.C. in Raleigh-Durham, N. Carolina

The New Age Study of Humanity's Purpose, Inc.
is a non-profit, educational organization committed to helping people reach their highest potential. We network with more than 7,000 organizations and individuals throughout the world that are working toward finding viable solutions for sustained World Peace and Planetary Healing.

We also sponsor the annual World Congress On Illumination, which is a global conference designed to bring the Light Beings of the world together to share our knowledge and wisdom as we fulfill the theme of: The Family of Humanity Creating a Unified Cup through which the Light of God will pour into the Planet Earth.

The New Age Study of Humanity's Purpose also organizes conferences, workshops and seminars throughout the world to provide people with tangible tools and personal experiences that will give them the courage and confidence they need to recognize their own self-worth. With a renewed sense of self-esteem, each person can Transform his or her Life into expressions of success, happiness and fulfillment beyond anything they ever believed possible.

If you would like to support our work, you tax-deductible contributions may be sent to:

The New Age Study of Humanity's Purpose
P.O. Box 41883
Tucson, AZ 85717
Phone 520-885-7909, Fax 520-751-3835

Your Love Offerings will be used solely to expand the Light of the World, and we ask the Universal Source of all Life to expand your gift a thousand-fold on its return to you.